This Little Explorer book belongs to:

_____

For
Curious Learners

Published by Grant Publishing

Sales and Enquires: grantpublishingltd@gmail.com

FOLLOW US ON SOCIAL MEDIA

@grantpublishingltd

60

FACTS

ABOUT

ITALY

60 Facts About Italy

Calling all young adventurers! Are you ready to immerse yourself in the captivating world of Italy, where ancient traditions and vibrant culture come to life? Prepare to be swept away on a journey of discovery through a land filled with majestic historical sites, delectable traditional cuisine, and a tapestry of fascinating customs.

In this enchanting book, you will uncover the secrets of Italy's extraordinary cultural heritage. Marvel at the breathtaking beauty of ancient Roman ruins and magnificent Renaissance art that adorn the landscape, each with its own unique story to tell. Delve into the realm of Italian inventors, whose ingenious creations have shaped the world we live in today.

For Parents

We know that reading a book about a new country can be an exciting adventure for your child. It's important to remember that kids need breaks and may not want to read the book all in one sitting. Encourage them to take breaks as needed, and ask them questions about what they've learned so far. Discussing the facts with your child can help them remember and retain the information better. You can also use the book as a springboard for further exploration and learning about Italy. Perhaps you can plan a family outing to try some Italian cuisine or visit a local museum with exhibits on Italian culture. Above all, we hope that this book sparks your child's curiosity and inspires them to learn more about the world around them.

MAP

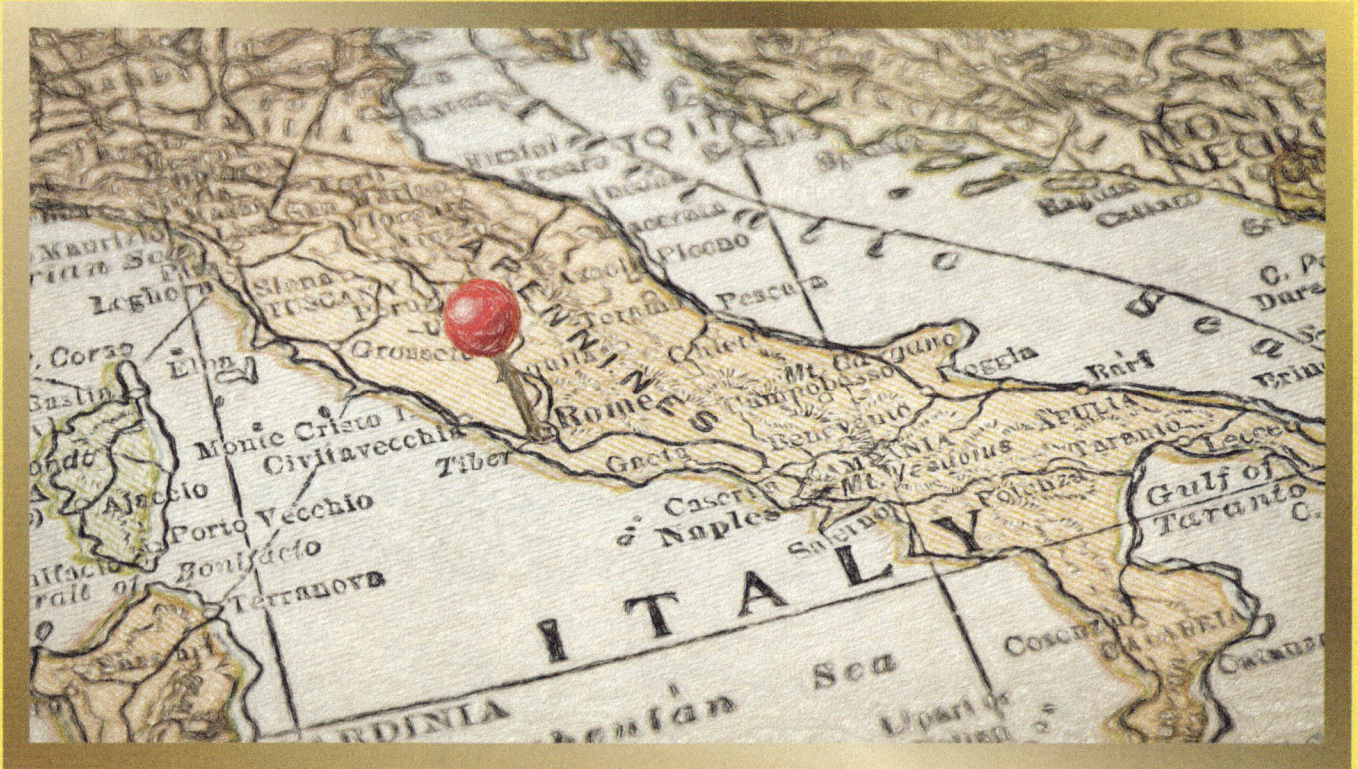

Contents

THE
COUNTRY

9

Italy is a country in the continent of Europe.

Italy boasts a diverse range of natural landscapes, from the stunning Amalfi Coast and the majestic Dolomites to the picturesque Tuscan countryside and the enchanting islands of Sicily and Sardinia.

Italy is situated in southern Europe, occupying the Apennine Peninsula and a number of islands, including Sicily and Sardinia, in the Mediterranean Sea.

Italy is often referred to as the "Land of Pasta and Pizza.

Italy is renowned for its delicious and diverse cuisine, which includes a wide variety of pasta dishes, pizzas, and many other culinary delights.

Italy shares land borders with six countries: France, Switzerland, Austria, Slovenia, San Marino, and Vatican City.

Piazza della Signoria

Italy is divided into 20 regions, each with its own unique culture and traditions. These regions are further subdivided into provinces and municipalities, creating a rich tapestry of local identities across the country.

POSTE ITALIANE L.20

Milan City

The capital city of Italy is Rome.

Italy is home to some of the world's most iconic historical sites, including the Colosseum in Rome, the ancient city of Pompeii, and the ruins of Herculaneum. These ancient treasures offer a window into the past, showcasing the grandeur of Roman civilization.

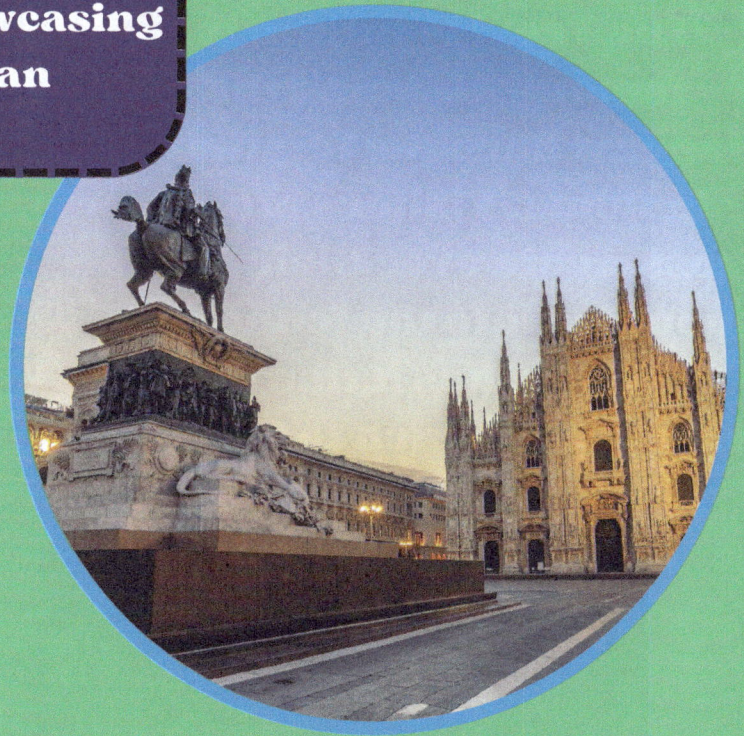

Milan Cathedral

Rome is famously known as the "City of Seven Hills." These hills include Aventine, Caelian, Capitoline, Esquiline, Palatine, Quirinal, and Viminal. Each hill has its own history and significance.

The Trevi Fountain is famous for being the largest Baroque fountain in Rome. Visitors often toss a coin over their left shoulder into the fountain, as legend has it that this ensures a return to Rome.

Trevi Fountain

Major cities in Italy include Milan, Rome, and Florence."

Italy is home to the world's oldest university, the University of Bologna, founded in 1088. It has a rich history of academic excellence and innovation.

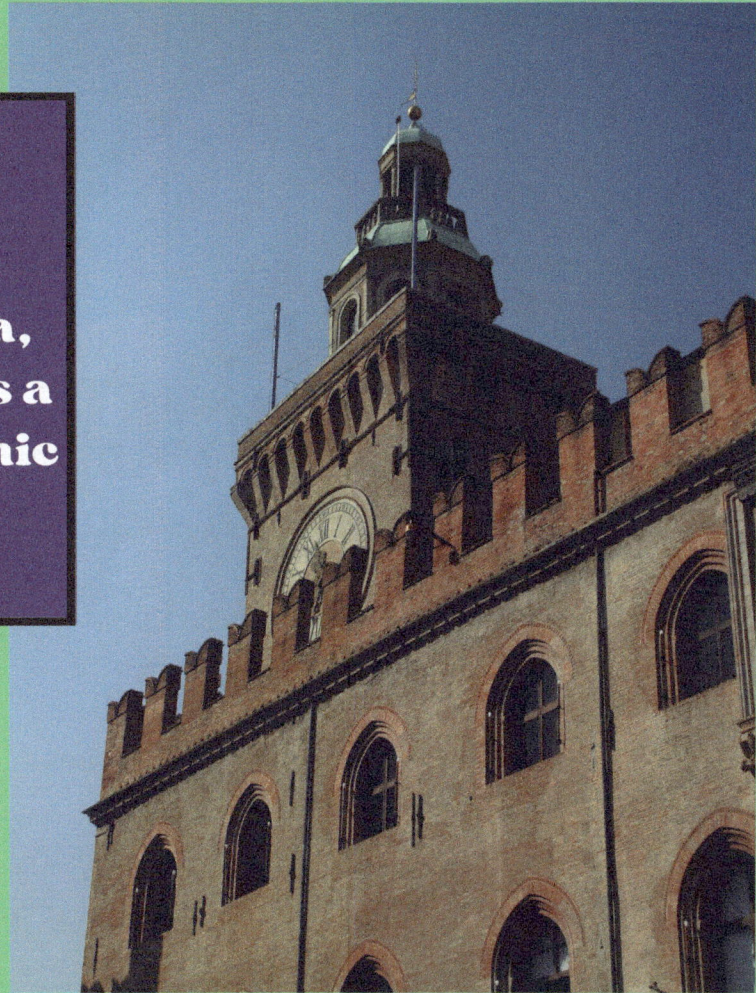

Picture of University of Bologna

The official language of Italy is Italian.

Here are some common phrases in Italian:
Hello - Ciao
Good morning - Buongiorno
Good afternoon - Buon pomeriggio
Good evening - Buona sera
Good night - Buona notte
Thank you - Grazie

Italian is spoken by an estimated 65 million people worldwide.

Italian is the official language spoken throughout Italy.

The national anthem of Italy is called "Il Canto degli Italiani," often referred to as the "Inno di Mameli" or "Fratelli d'Italia."

There are over 350 types of pasta produced in the country. From spaghetti and penne to farfalle and orecchiette, Italian pasta offers a wide range of shapes and sizes to suit various dishes and tastes.

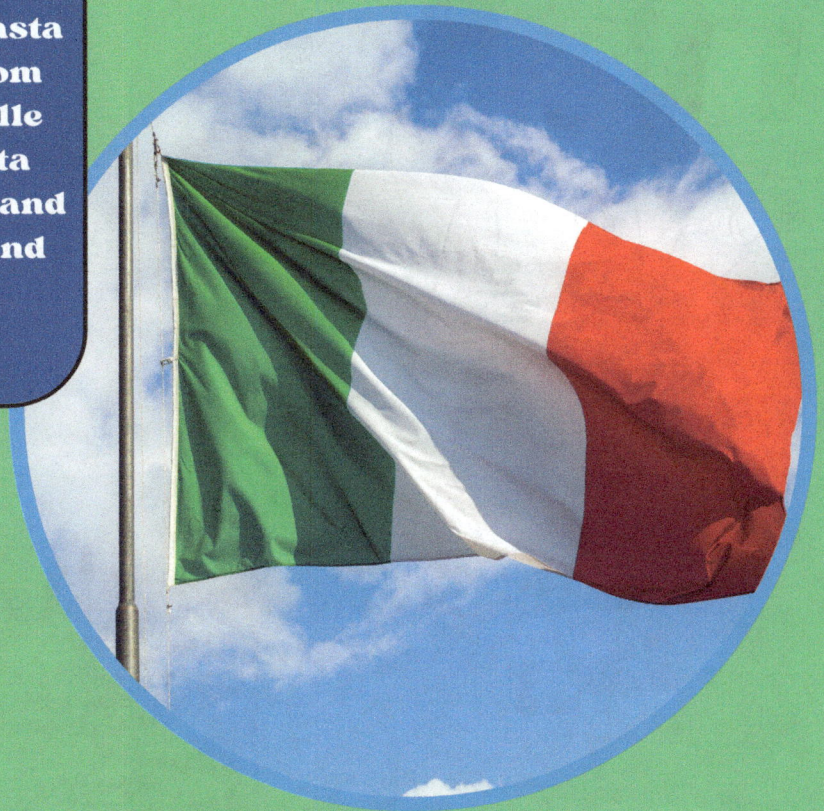

Picture of Italian national flag

Italy has a population of approximately 60 million people, making it one of the most populous countries in Europe.

Italy is the fifth most populous country in Europe, after Russia, Germany, United Kingdom and France.

Italy is the 25th most populated country in the world, with a population of nearly 60 million people.

Italy covers an area of approximately 301,340 square kilometers.

Tuscany is considered the birthplace of the Italian Renaissance, a cultural and artistic movement that had a profound impact on Europe.

Old street in San Gimignano

Italy is the 71st largest country in the world.

Italy is renowned for its rich cultural heritage, boasting the highest number of UNESCO World Heritage Sites globally, including iconic landmarks like the Colosseum, Venice, and the historic center of Rome.

The historic center of Rome

People from Italy are called Italian.

The currency used in Italy is the Euro (€).

In Italy, people drive on the right side of the road.

The national flag of Ukraine is bicolour consisting of equally sized horizontal bands of blue and yellow.

The Italian national flag, known as the Tricolore, was officially adopted on January 7, 1797.

The Italian national flag, or Tricolore, consists of three vertical bands of equal width. The colors of the flag are green, white, and red, which are associated with Italy's rich history and culture. Green symbolizes hope, white represents faith, and red stands for charity. These colors are often seen as embodying the essence of the Italian nation and its values.

Italy is a founding member of the United Nations.

Picture of the United Nations Office in
Geneva

Italy is indeed a member of the World Trade Organization (WTO), the Council of Europe, and the Organization for Security and Co-operation in Europe (OSCE).

Picture of a the World Trade Organisation building in Geneva. Switzerland.

HISTORY

During ancient times, Italy was inhabited by various peoples, including the Etruscans, who lived in the central part of the Italian Peninsula, and the Romans, who eventually established the Roman Empire.

The Romans played a significant role in shaping Italy's history and culture.

During the Roman Republic and Empire, which lasted for several centuries, Italy was a central part of the ancient world. It was home to the influential Roman civilization, known for its advancements in governance, engineering, and culture.

On 24th June 1946, Italy became a republic after a national referendum, abolishing the monarchy that had ruled for centuries.

CULTURE

The largest religion in Italy is Christianity, predominantly Roman Catholicism.

Grand Canal Venice

Italian customs are heavily influenced by Roman Catholicism, which plays a significant role in the country's culture and traditions.

Picture of Orthodox church in Church of Saint Benedict in Catania, Sicily

Italy has a significant Roman Catholic population, making it one of the countries with the largest Roman Catholic communities in the world.

Italy is predominantly Roman Catholic, and the country is home to the Vatican City, the spiritual center of the Roman Catholic Church, led by the Pope.

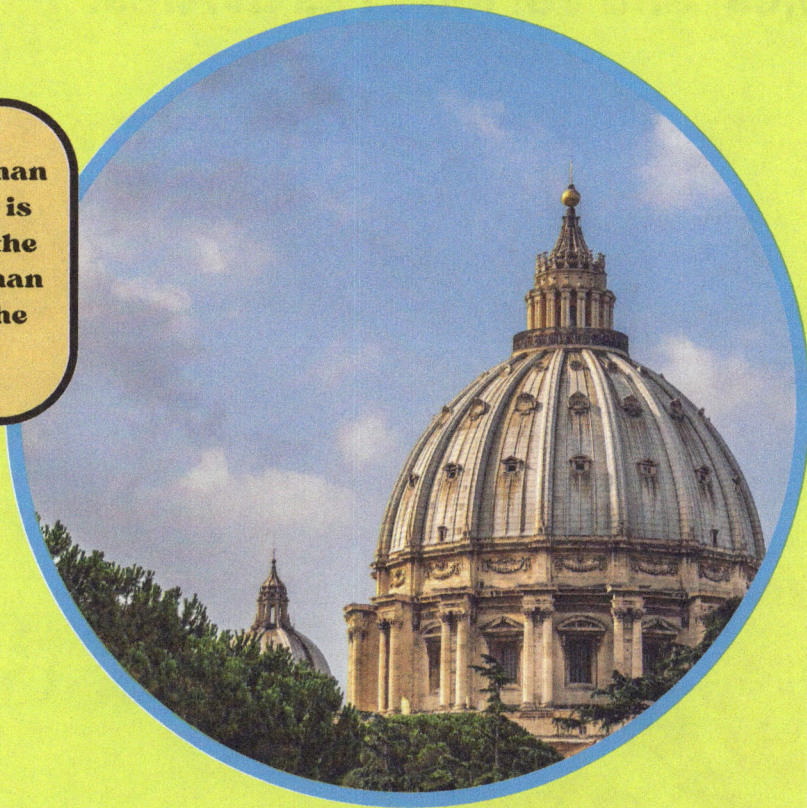

Picture of The Vatican

In Italy, one of the biggest holidays is Ferragosto, celebrated on August 15th. It marks the peak of the summer season and is a day for relaxation, picnics, and various festivities.

In Italy, the tradition of Easter eggs, known as "uova di Pasqua," also has ancient roots and is a significant part of Easter celebrations. These eggs are often elaborately decorated and exchanged as gifts among family members and friends.

Picture of Ukrainian Pysanky eggs

Italian literature has a rich and influential history, with renowned authors like Dante Alighieri, Petrarch, and Boccaccio making significant contributions to world literature. Dante's "Divine Comedy" is a masterpiece of Italian literature and has had a profound impact on Western literary traditions.

Dante Alighieri, often referred to simply as Dante, was a renowned Italian poet of the Late Middle Ages. He is best known for his epic work, "The Divine Comedy," which is considered one of the greatest literary achievements of all time.

Portrait of Dante Alighieri

Italy is one of the most successful countries in the Eurovision Song Contest, with multiple victories and a rich history of participation since its debut in 1956.

Italy has participated in Eurovision since the contest's inception in 1956. The country has won the competition twice, first in 1964 with Gigliola Cinquetti's "Non ho l'età" and then in 1990 with Toto Cutugno's "Insieme: 1992." Italy has hosted Eurovision twice, in 1965 (Naples) and 1991 (Rome).

Artisan textile arts play an important role in Italian culture, especially in various Italian regional traditions and festivals.

Football is one of the most popular sports in Italy and holds a special place in the hearts of Italians.

Italy has a strong tradition in cycling, with the Giro d'Italia being one of the most prestigious cycling races globally. Tennis, motorsport, basketball, and rugby also have dedicated followings in the country, reflecting Italy's diverse sports culture.

The Italian national football team has won the FIFA World Cup four times (in 1934, 1938, 1982, and 2006), making them one of the most successful teams in the tournament's history.

One of the country's beloved activities is bocce, a traditional Italian bowling game that has been played for centuries.

Italian music encompasses a rich and diverse range of styles, from classical opera to contemporary pop and rock.

Italy has made immense contributions to the world of classical music, with legendary composers like Giuseppe Verdi and Giacomo Puccini creating timeless operas.

In the modern era, Italian pop and rock music have also achieved international acclaim, with artists such as Luciano Pavarotti, Andrea Bocelli, and Eros Ramazzotti captivating global audiences.

Italy has also been the birthplace of numerous renowned composers throughout its rich musical history. Some of the world's most celebrated classical composers, such as Antonio Vivaldi, Giuseppe Verdi, and Giacomo Puccini, hailed from Italy.

Vivaldi

CLIMATE

Italy enjoys a diverse climate with regions experiencing Mediterranean, alpine, and continental climates depending on the location, making it an attractive destination for tourists.

Positano Resort in Italy

The weather in Italy features a wide range of climates, from the sunny Mediterranean coasts to the snow-covered Alps in the north. Rainfall and sunshine vary throughout the country, offering diverse experiences for travelers.

The wettest months in Italy typically occur in the late autumn and early winter, from October to December, with some regional variations across the country.

Italian summer holidays -Pizzo Calabro - beautiful coastal town in Calabria Italy

Italy boasts approximately 1,500 rivers within its borders.

A fun fact about Italy's rivers is that the Po River, the longest river in Italy, is often referred to as the "River of Love" due to its romantic associations in Italian literature and poetry.

Smiling Tourist Traveling in Italy

The Po River is Italy's longest river.

The Po River is that it is often referred to as the "River of the Italian Poets" because many renowned Italian poets, including Dante Alighieri, Petrarch, and Lord Byron, have drawn inspiration from its scenic beauty and cultural significance.

The Po River

Italy boasts a number of beautiful lakes, and Lake Garda, the largest in the country, is particularly notable.

Lake Garda also offers a variety of recreational activities, from water sports to hiking, making it a popular destination for both tourists and locals.

Picture of Lake Garda

The country's national emblem prominently features the Emblem of Italy, which includes a five-pointed star, a cogwheel, and an olive branch.

Italy has a diverse range of insect, bird, and mammal species.

Common animals found in Italy include foxes, wild cats, martens, deer, wild boars, rodents, and chamois.

Italy has a rich tradition of textile art, including intricate embroidery, with each region showcasing its unique patterns and styles.

Mount Gran Paradiso is the highest mountain in Italy.

CUISINE

The national dish of Italy is pasta. Italian cuisine is famous for its wide variety of pasta dishes, from classic spaghetti with tomato sauce to more elaborate options like lasagna, ravioli, and linguine with seafood.

Pasta is typically prepared with fresh, high-quality ingredients, and the sauce choices are diverse, ranging from creamy Alfredo to hearty Bolognese.

Italy offers a delectable array of dishes, from pasta and pizza to rich desserts like tiramisu. Its culinary heritage is a testament to the country's love for food, featuring iconic flavors that have become beloved worldwide.

Popular drinks in Italy include espresso, cappuccino, and various types of wine, such as Chianti, Barolo, and Prosecco. Italy is also known for its iconic cocktails like the Negroni and Aperol Spritz.

Italy is one of the leading wine producers in the world, known for its high-quality wines such as Chianti, Barolo, and Prosecco, which are exported globally.

Glossary

Italy: A country located in Southern Europe, celebrated for its rich history, art, culture, and stunning landscapes.

Rome: The capital and largest city of Italy, renowned for its ancient history, iconic landmarks such as the Colosseum and Roman Forum, and Vatican City, an independent city-state within its borders.

Pizza: A beloved Italian dish consisting of a thin, round crust topped with tomato sauce, cheese, and various toppings. Pizza is an internationally renowned symbol of Italian cuisine.

Dolomites: A mountain range located in Northern Italy, known for its dramatic peaks, hiking trails, and winter sports opportunities.

Venice: A unique city in northeastern Italy.

Sistine Chapel: A renowned chapel within Vatican City, located in Rome, Italy, famous for its stunning ceiling painted by Michelangelo, including the iconic image of the "Creation of Adam."

Gelato: A delightful Italian frozen dessert similar to ice cream, known for its rich flavors and creamy texture. Gelato is a beloved treat enjoyed by locals and visitors alike.

Amalfi Coast: A picturesque stretch of coastline along the southern edge of Italy's Sorrentine Peninsula, known for its dramatic cliffs, charming villages, and stunning sea views.

Leonardo da Vinci: An Italian Renaissance polymath known for his contributions to art, science, and invention. Leonardo's works, including the "Mona Lisa" and "The Last Supper," are celebrated worldwide.

Author's Note

Dear young readers,

I'm thrilled to have had the opportunity to introduce you to the enchanting country of Italy, a land brimming with history, art, and culture. As an author, I'm constantly inspired by the remarkable diversity and splendor of our world, and I hope that this book has ignited your curiosity and encouraged you to delve deeper into the wonders of Italy.

I penned this book with the belief that learning about diverse cultures and countries enriches our understanding of the world. Embracing and respecting different traditions and ways of life is crucial, and I trust that this book has allowed you to do just that.

If you found joy in reading this book, I'd greatly appreciate it if you could leave a review on Amazon. Reviews play a significant role in helping fellow readers discover books and can make a meaningful impact, especially for independent authors like myself.

Thank you for embarking on this literary journey with me, and I hope that it has kindled your sense of curiosity and wonder. Keep exploring and expanding your knowledge of the world around you!

Warm regards,
Grant Publishng